2-4-96

A Dorling Kindersley Book

Project Editor Linda Martin
Art Editors Anita Ruddell and Peter Bailey
Photography Clive Streeter

First published in Great Britain in 1991 by Dorling
Kindersley Publishers Limited, 9 Henrietta Street,
London WC2E 8PS

Copyright © 1991 *illustrations* Dorling Kindersley
Limited, London
Copyright © 1991 *text* Neil Ardley

**British Library Cataloguing in Publication Data
is available**

ISBN 0-86317-507-X

Reproduced in Hong Kong by Bright Arts
Typeset by Windsorgraphics, Ringwood, Hampshire
Printed in Belgium by Proost

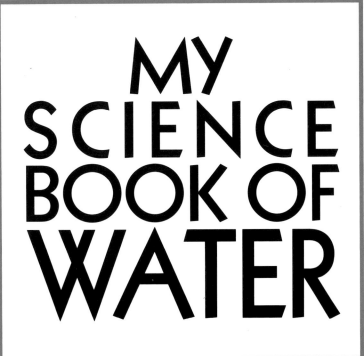

MY
SCIENCE
BOOK OF
WATER

Written by
Neil Ardley

Dorling Kindersley • London

What is water ?

Water is wonderful stuff. Apart from being fun to swim in, it is essential for life. All living things need water to survive. In fact, we can survive longer without food than without water to drink! Although we normally think of water as a liquid, it has two other forms. When it freezes solid, it becomes ice. When it is boiled, it becomes a gas called water vapour, which disappears into the air.

The power of water
Water can change the shape of the land. The force of waves battering against the shore will eventually wear away the rocks, causing the cliffs to change shape.

Mostly water
Did you know that more than half of your weight is the weight of the water in your body? The water in these buckets is the same as the amount of water in this girl's body!

Watery world
Water is almost everywhere. Oceans and seas cover nearly three-quarters of the Earth's surface.

Snow play
When water freezes, it becomes ice or snow.

Wet weather
Water affects the weather. When there is too much water vapour in the clouds, it rains!

⚠️ This sign means **take care.** You should ask an adult to help you with this step of the experiment.

Be a safe scientist
Follow all the directions carefully and always take care, especially with glass, scissors, matches, candles, and electricity. Never put anything in your mouth or eyes.

You can make a mess with water, so remember to clean up and dry everything when you have finished the experiment.

Water weight-lifter

Impress your friends with your strength! Ask them to lift a heavy bag of stones. They will find it difficult. But you can lift it easily – with the help of some water.

You will need:

Jug of water

Stones Large plastic bowl Plastic carrier bag

1 Put the stones into the plastic bag. Ask a friend to lift the bag. It takes a lot of effort.

2 Take out the stones. Put the plastic bag into the bowl. Now fill the bag with the stones again.

3 Pour some water into the bowl. Be careful not to let any go into the bag.

4 Now lift the bag of stones. This time it is easier. The bag is much lighter.

The water pushes up underneath the bag of stones. It supports the bag.

Water support
You are less heavy in water because the water supports your body. This support allows people recovering from injury to move around more easily in water. They can exercise and play in the water.

Floating and sinking

Why do big, heavy things like ships float, but small objects sink in the water? It all depends on how much water an object pushes out of the way, or "displaces". Objects that displace lots of water receive a strong upward push from the water. This push can support the object so that it floats.

1 Drop the marbles into the water. They sink to the bottom. Now drop the ball of plasticine into the water.

2 The plasticine ball also sinks. Neither the marbles nor the ball push much water out of the way. This means there is not enough upward push from the water to support them.

3 Remove the marbles and plasticine from the water. Shape the plasticine into a boat.

The heavy boat gets more push from the water as it sinks lower - enough to keep it afloat.

4 Put the plasticine back into the water. Now it floats! The boat is larger than the ball, so it pushes more water out of the way. This means it receives a strong upward push from the water underneath.

5 Add a "cargo" of marbles. The boat sinks lower in the water, but still floats.

Ships at sea
A large ship pushes a lot of water out of the way, so it gets a very strong upward push from the sea.

Liquid levels

Can liquids float or sink? And do things float or sink in liquids other than water? Test some to find out. It all depends on their "density". A dense liquid is heavier than the same amount of a less dense liquid.

You will need:

Tall, clear container

Grape

Jug of water

Syrup

Cooking oil

Cork

Plastic building block

Oil is lighter, or less dense than syrup.

Water is denser than oil, but less dense than syrup.

1 Pour the syrup into the container.

2 Pour in the same amount of oil. It floats on the syrup.

3 Now add the same amount of cold water. It sinks through the oil but floats on the syrup.

4 Put the cork, plastic block, and the grape in the container.

The cork floats on oil.

The plastic block sinks in oil but floats on water.

The grape sinks in oil and water but floats on syrup.

5 The objects float at different levels, depending on how dense they are.

Oil at sea
Oil that spills from a tanker floats on the sea because the oil is lighter, or less dense, than sea water. Much of the oil is washed ashore by the tide. This makes the beach very dirty, so it has to be thoroughly cleaned.

Water volcano

Did you know that one kind of water can float on top of another? You can see this for yourself by making a "volcano" erupt under water.

You will need:

Jug

Small bottle with cap

Ink or food colouring

Glass tank or bowl

1 Pour cold water into the tank until it is about three-quarters full.

2 ⚠ Fill the bottle with hot tap water. Add a few drops of ink or food colouring.

Make sure the ink or food colouring is well mixed into the water.

3 Screw the cap back on and shake the bottle well.

Water "expands" - takes up more space - when it is heated. This makes it lighter than cold water.

4 Place the bottle on the bottom of the tank and unscrew the cap.

5 The hot water from the bottle is lighter, or less "dense" than the cold water, so it shoots to the top of the tank.

6 The hot coloured water forms a layer on top of the cold water. As it cools, the coloured water mixes with the cold water.

Hot-water holes
A column of hot water shoots up from a vent or hole in the ocean floor, far below the surface.

Leaping water

Does water some-times flow uphill? You can build a fountain and find out how to make water leap high in the air.

You will need:

Plastic tubing

Pin

Sticky tape

Funnel

Jug of water

Hold the sealed end of the tube above the funnel.

1 Put the funnel in one end of the tube. Seal the other end tightly with sticky tape. Make a small hole in the tape with the pin.

2 Pour enough water into the funnel to fill the tube.

3 Hold the tube over a sink and slightly lower the sealed end. Water begins to flow from the pinhole.

The weight of the water pushes it out of the tube and up into the air.

4 Now lower the sealed end further. Water shoots upward from the hole, just like a fountain.

Fountain power
Water flows from a lake high in the hills to feed this fountain. Because the lake water is higher than the fountain, its weight pushes the fountain water into the air.

Deep-water diver

How do submarines dive and return to the surface? With just a few simple objects, you can make your own toy "diver". This diver will sink and rise in a bottle of water, in just the same way that a submarine dives and surfaces in the sea.

Plastic
pen top

Glass of
water

Plasticine

Thin, clear
plastic bottle

If your pen top has a hole in the tip, seal it with plasticine.

1 Stick a small piece of plasticine on to the pen top. This is the diver.

The diver should just float.

Air inside the pen top makes it float.

2 Put the diver into a glass of water. Remove or add plasticine until the diver floats upright.

3 Completely fill the bottle with water. Put the diver in and screw the top on tightly.

Water is forced into the pen top. This makes it heavy and it sinks.

Water leaves the pen top. This makes it lighter and it rises.

4 Squeeze the bottle hard. The diver sinks to the bottom.

5 Let go of the bottle. Now the diver rises to the top again.

Underwater exploration
Submarines and underwater vessels that explore the ocean depths contain special tanks that are flooded with sea water to make them dive. Pumping air into the tanks to remove the water makes the vessels lighter, and they rise to the surface.

Speedboats

Make a boat that shoots forward when you touch the surface of the water behind it. It shows that water has a strong force called "surface tension" that pulls at things floating on water. The pulling power helps water to wash things clean.

You will need:

Large, clean bowl of water

Coloured card

Washing-up liquid

Pencil

Ruler

Scissors

1 Draw a simple boat shape on the piece of coloured card.

2 Carefully cut out the boat and float it on the water in the bowl.

3 Put a drop of washing-up liquid on your finger.

20

4 When the water is still, gently touch the water behind the boat with your finger. The boat shoots forward.

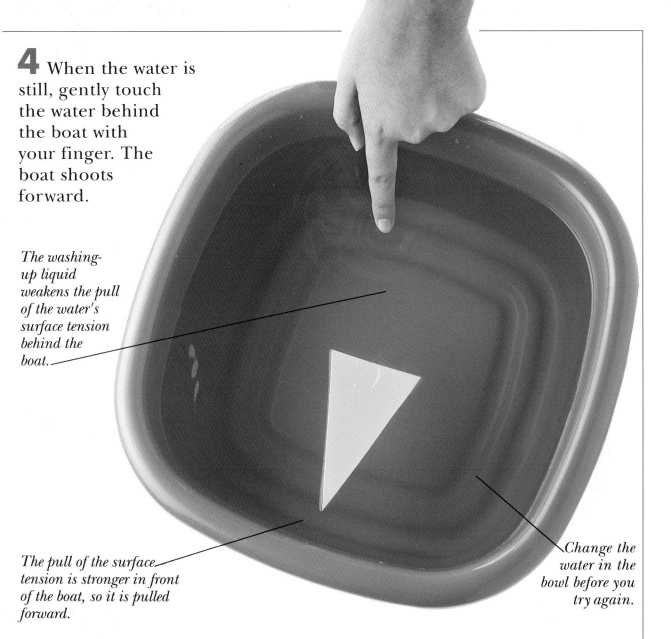

The washing-up liquid weakens the pull of the water's surface tension behind the boat.

The pull of the surface tension is stronger in front of the boat, so it is pulled forward.

Change the water in the bowl before you try again.

Washing dishes
Washing-up liquid helps water to get dirty dishes clean. It weakens the grip with which dirt and grease stick to dishes. This makes it easier for the water to pull the dirt and grease off during washing.

Vanishing water

Do you know what happens to the water in wet clothes when they are hung up to dry? This simple experiment will show you what happens to it and how water disappears, or "evaporates", into thin air.

You will need:

Saucer   Jug of water   Glass bowl

Pen

Small glass

1 Mark a line on the glass with the pen.

2 Pour water into the glass up to the mark.

Take care not to spill any water.

3 Pour the water from the glass into the saucer.

4 Fill the glass with water to the mark again.

5 Cover the glass with the bowl. Leave both the saucer and the covered glass in a warm place.

The water level does not fall. The water vapour cannot escape as it is trapped by the bowl.

Water evaporates more quickly when it is warm.

6 The water in the saucer eventually vanishes. Water that is open to the air forms water vapour, which is invisible. This mixes with the air and is carried away.

Wet washing
When wet clothes are hung up to dry, the water changes into invisible water vapour that mixes with the air. Gradually all the water evaporates and the clothes become dry.

Water from nowhere

Why do drops of water appear on plants on cold mornings, even when it has not been raining? By cooling some air, you can show that the water comes out of thin air! This will also show you how clouds, mist, and fog form in the air.

You will need:

Ice cubes

Rolling pin

Card

Tea towel

Glass

1 Wrap some ice cubes in the tea towel.

Press down firmly on the ice with the rolling pin. There is no need to bang it hard!

2 Crush the ice cubes with the rolling pin. You may need an adult to do this for you.

3 Tip the crushed ice into the glass, which must be completely dry.

4 Cover the glass with the card and wait for a few minutes.

5 The side of the glass goes misty. Run a finger round the glass. It is wet.

Tiny drops of water appear on the side of the glass.

The ice cools the glass and the air around it. Cold air cannot hold much water vapour, so some vapour changes into drops of water.

Early morning dew
On a cold morning, the air cannot hold much water vapour. Some of it changes into tiny drops of water, called dew, where the air meets the cold ground. Clouds, mist, and fog contain tiny drops of water that form and float in cold air.

Catch a cube

Challenge a friend to lift an ice cube with a piece of thread without tying a knot or touching the cube. It seems impossible, but you can do it easily.

You will need:

Salt

Ice cubes

Thick thread

1 Soak the thread in water and lay it on top of the ice cube.

2 Sprinkle some salt all along the thread. Wait for about 30 seconds.

The salt makes some of the ice turn to water.

3 Lift the thread and up comes the ice cube!

The coldness of the ice freezes the water again, trapping the thread in the cube.

Safety in the snow
A snowy or icy road is dangerous because it is very slippery. Putting salt on the road turns the ice or snow to water, and makes the road safe for traffic.

Ice needs space

See how water grows, or "expands", when it freezes to ice. Nothing can stop it taking up more space. Ice can even burst metal pipes.

You will need

Water

Aluminium foil

Funnel

Small, thick glass or plastic bottle

1 Using the funnel and jug, completely fill the bottle with water.

Use a bottle with a narrow neck.

2 Cover the bottle *loosely* with foil. Put it in the freezer. Leave the water to freeze solid.

There is not enough room in the bottle for all the ice, so some sticks out of the top.

3 ⚠ As the ice forms, it pushes up the foil. Be careful, the glass may crack.

Protecting pipes
In very cold weather, water inside pipes may freeze. As it expands, the ice can burst the pipe. Wrapping cloth around pipes helps to stop water freezing.

Funny flowers

We normally think of water flowing downwards, but it can flow upwards! By making some flowers change colour, you will see how plants obtain the water they need to live.

You will need:

Two fresh white flowers

Celery with leaves

Scissors

Three glasses of water

Green, red and blue food colouring

1 Add a different food colouring to each glass of water.

2 Carefully split the stem of one flower to just under the flower head.

Trim the ends of each stem.

3 Put each half of the split-stemmed flower in a different glass. Put the flower with the whole stem in the third glass.

The whole stem feeds green water to all the petals of this flower.

The split stem feeds red water to this half of the flower.

The split stem feeds blue water to this half of the flower.

4 Put the flowers in a warm room. After a few hours, they begin to change colour. They suck up the coloured water, which travels up the stem to the petals.

5 Trim the end of the celery and put it in a glass of red water. The water travels up the stem to the leaves and they turn red.

If you cut across the celery, you can see the veins that carry the water to the leaves.

Picture credits
(Picture credits abbreviation key: B=below, C=centre, L=left, R=right, T=top)

Brian Cosgrove: 7CR; Derbyshire Countryside Ltd/Andy Williams: 17BC; Pete Gardner: 6BC, 7TL; Malvin Van Gelderen: 23BL; Sally and Richard Greenhill: 9CL; The Image Bank: 6TR; NHPA/Manfred Danegger: 25BL; Science Photo Library/Adam Hart-Davis: 26BL; Ron Church: 19BL; M Fraudreau Rapho: 13BL; Peter Ryan/Scripps: 15BR; Spectrum Colour Library: 27BL; Zefa: 7TR, 11BR, 21BL

Picture research Kate Fox

Title page photography Dave King

Dorling Kindersley would like to thank Claire Gillard for editorial assistance and Mark Regardsoe for design assistance; Mrs Bradbury, the staff and children of Allfarthing Junior School, Wandsworth, especially Melanie Best; Nadia Agadia, Katie Martin and Kate Whiteway.